At The End Of The Day is a journal for your travels through the end of the day! Add your thoughts At The End Of The Day...

At The End Of The Day...

Dr. Rochelle Newton

At The End Of The Day... How do you approach your day determines the day

Good days are days that begin with a good attitude regardless of what is ahead of you. If you start the day believing the worst is coming, the worst is coming. Start the day knowing you will conquer the days' dilemmas. Changing how you see your day, changes your day.

At The End Of The Day...

Did you change how you started your day?

_____

_____

_____

What changed about your day?

_____

_____

_____

At The End Of The Day... You have overcome so much

You will overcome much more! There are some days you may question the accuracy of your strength. However, when you look over your life, you should be amazed at your accomplishments. The ups and downs of your life should remind you of the grace of your strength. You are movement in style. Push forward.

At The End Of The Day...

What was your greatest obstacle?

_____

_____

_____

How did you feel when you overcame that obstacle?

_____

_____

_____

At The End Of The Day... You are perfect just as you are

We know no one is perfect. However, the you the Universe has made is perfect as is. Look into the mirror and say I am beautiful and say it daily. The little girl or boy inside of you needs you to love to see the beautiful you. We may get lost in life but remind yourself of who you are. You are the Universe's gift!

At The End Of The Day...

Do you know how loved you are?

_____

_____

_____

What is your favorite thing about you?

_____

_____

_____

*At The End Of The Day...*Look forward, not backward

There is an adage that says, 'You cannot drive a car looking backward.' There is some logic to examining the past. However, there is no logic to living in your past. Your future is in front of you, not behind you. Let the past go. Gather the good and move forward.

At The End Of The Day...

Have you found value looking backward?

_____

_____

_____

List three things you see in your future.

_____

_____

_____

*At The End Of The Day...*Count your wins, not your losses

When the losses seem to rule the day, it is easy to focus on them. They divert your attention from the things that really need your attention. Every time you win, celebrate it. A win is a win. Even the little wins. The more you celebrate, the wins, the more you will win.

At The End Of The Day...

What was your last win?

_____
_____
_____

How do you celebrate your wins?

_____
_____
_____

At The End Of The Day... Admire the world around you

The Universe made everything you see, and everything is beautiful as it ages. As time evolves, everything changes. Many times, we are in a hurry to get the latest of everything. The beauty is in the aged. As seasons change, people age, and things go out of style, beauty lives on. Beauty is within and without and it never dies.

At The End Of The Day...

Do you see beauty around you?

_____

_____

_____

List three beautiful things around you including you.

_____

_____

_____

*At The End Of The Day…*Is what you are doing serving you

If so, continue. If not, do something different. *Einstein said, "Insanity is doing the same thing repeatedly and expecting different results."* Yet, we do it every day. Look into yourself and find those things that do not serve you and stop doing them and do things that serve you.

At The End Of The Day...

List something not serving you.

_____

_____

_____

List something serving you.

_____

_____

_____

At The End Of The Day... Like glass, you are fragile, but you are strong

Our bodies are subject to physical injury, health scares, and other damages. Yet, with all that can go wrong, our bodies are strong. We recover, rebuild, and get better. We play sports, run marathons, and exercise. We have children. We invent. We change. We grow. It is amazing to be human. We are resilient!

At The End Of The Day...

Do you recognize your strength?

_____

_____

_____

Do you know the importance of rest in recovery?

_____

_____

_____

At The End Of The Day... There is nothing you cannot do if you believe you can

Doubt is a powerful emotion, and it lurks in the back of our minds. You must believe in yourself and your dreams and thoughts. You must force doubt out of your mind. The story of I think I can is so important. You can. You can. You can! You must win the battle of 'I can' over the battle over 'I cannot' or doubt.

At The End Of The Day...

Do you doubt yourself?

_____

_____

_____

I believe in you! List what you believe about yourself.

_____

_____

_____

At The End Of The Day... You know the difference between right and wrong

There is this little voice always talking to us. When you have a choice between right and wrong, the voice is always there. In every decision, in every choice, and everything. We can choose not to listen, but we know. When you choose, choose right. Do the right thing. It is better for us all. What do you choose?

At The End Of The Day...

Do you listen to the little voices (You are not crazy)?

_____

_____

_____

How often do you choose right over wrong*?*

_____

_____

_____

At The End Of The Day... You are smart

Some narratives are often told to put some down and lift others up. These narratives harm those who are put down. A doctor once said to me, "You see that diploma on the wall, I barely passed but I passed." The definition of smart is subjective. You are smart. What you achieved is more important than how you achieved it.

At The End Of The Day...

Do you know how smart you are?

_____

_____

_____

List your brilliance.

_____

_____

_____

At The End Of The Day... Rainy days are always coming

Do you save for the rainy day or live for today? Conservative logic says save for it. Money is a tool. It should be used to pay your bills, save for your future, and create what is next. When you plan to retire, have enough money to retire. I say, divide the dollar. $.33 for your bills, $.33 for you, and $.34 for saving.

At The End Of The Day...

Are you a saver or a spender?
_____
_____
_____

Learn about money early.
_____
_____
_____

At The End Of The Day...Are you engaged in your life?

Often, we watch our lives like they are quarters (childhood, adolescence, adulthood, and old age), in a game. If you are having troubles, ask for help. There is no shame in asking for help. Engage in your life. Do not shut your eyes when you encounter challenges. Open your eyes and face them head-on. It is your life. Own it!

At The End Of The Day...

Are you engaged with your life?
_____
_____
_____

Do you ask for help when you need it?
_____
_____
_____

*At The End Of The Day...*If you look beyond the tip of your nose, you might find the world

Many times, the world is just what we know. Most of us live near our parents. Venture beyond your block, your city, or your state. Go visit a friend, a relative, or anyone in a different area. Look at a map and pinpoint somewhere you would like to go and go. Try something new. Change is good.

At The End Of The Day...

Have you traveled beyond the neighborhood where you grew up?

_____
_____

Will you travel outside of your head?

_____
_____

At The End Of The Day... You should feel safe

One thing that should be a constant in our lives is safety. If you do not feel safe, please tell someone. Loving ourselves contributes to safety. You should not feel ashamed to ask for help. Someone in your life will help you. Find that trusted family member or friend and tell them. Please get help!

The End Of The Day... Help is available

24-hour help

For the **Suicide Prevention Lifeline**, call 800-273-8255

For the **Domestic Violence Hotline**, 800-799-7233

Call 911 if you or the person you are helping is in immediate danger.

*At The End Of The Day...*Love is love every day, all day, and all night

Love has been defined by many. The only definition that matters is yours. Love should care for your soul. The love you receive in the day should be equal to or greater than the love you receive in the night. Love looks love through all things.

At The End Of The Day...

Do you Love you?

_____
_____
_____

If you do not love yourself, you may not recognize love when it comes.

_____
_____
_____

At The End Of The Day... Airlines suggest you secure yourself before you secure your child

Why do you think this is? Because, if you do not take care of yourself first, you cannot take care of anyone else. We do this so often; that we forget how to love ourselves. Through the years, self-love wanes. Take care of yourself.

At The End Of The Day...

What is the nicest thing you have done for yourself?

_____

_____

_____

Are you your most important person?

_____

_____

_____

At The End Of The Day... Be wary of technology

When technology is free, you are the product. Sometimes technology is not what it seems. It is the Little Red Riding Hood story, wolves cloaked in sheep's clothing. Be careful in this digital world. There is more danger than we know. Before you click, open, or send, know.

At The End of The Day...

Are you familiar with technology?

_____

_____

_____

What free technology do you use?

_____

_____

_____

*At The End Of The Day...*If the idea came to you, do not let it die

That idea was meant for you. You can ignore it or think it is too big or too small, but it is your idea. Act upon it. All the great innovations in the world were someone's idea. And guess what? They acted upon it. So, are you going to let your idea die? The Universe gave you that idea.

At The End Of The Day...

What do you do when ideas come to mind?

_____
_____
_____

How do you act upon those ideas?

_____
_____
_____

At The End Of The Day... Friends should be friends

That does not mean they are perfect. We all have ups and downs. However, through all the hard times, friends should be there. Give yourself and your friends grace. But if they repeatedly fail you, let them go. If they are needy or are draining, you may need to rethink that friendship.

At The End Of The Day...

Do you have friends that are always there?

_____
_____
_____

Are you there for your friends?

_____
_____
_____

*At The End Of The Day...*It does not hurt to say, I am sorry

I am sorry is hard for some to say. However, these three words heal. You will be amazed at what they can do. You may feel saying I am sorry is not necessary, but you may be wrong. Do not rely on your thinking. Just say you are sorry.

At The End Of The Day...

Have you felt uncomfortable saying you were sorry?

_____
_____
_____

Were you owed an apology and did not receive it?

_____
_____
_____

*At The End Of The Day...*There is a difference between I love you and love you

I love you is intentional. It has become common to say, 'Love you'. We say it in passing with no eye contact. What is the difference between I love you and love you? I love you is an emotional connection to someone and love you is a passing emotion.

At The End Of The Day...

Do you make a difference between I love you and love you?

_____

_____

_____

Do you prefer I love you or love you?

_____

_____

_____

At The End Of The Day... Eye contact is commitment

We shake hands on business deals and make eye contact. When we see someone who looks familiar, we make eye contact. Eye contact in many ways is a commitment to each other, not in a romantic manner but just to acknowledge each other.

At The End Of Day...

Do you think eye contact has an intent?

_____
_____
_____

Are you comfortable making eye contact?

_____
_____
_____

At The End Of The Day... Our planet does not have one of anything

There is not one type of tree, dog, or one type of anything. People are different from each other, and these differences are what make our planet beautiful. See the differences. You may learn something about yourself.

At The End Of The Day...

Do you see differences in animals, people, and trees around you?

_____

_____

_____

Do you appreciate the differences around you?

_____

_____

_____

At The End Of The Day...
Question everything

Sometimes we become comfortable with our daily routine. We start work, or we eat at a certain time. Often, we move about our lives with blinders on. Take time to see what surrounds us. Do not assume.

At The End Of The Day...

Do you follow a daily routine?

_____

_____

_____

Do you question things?

_____

_____

_____

At The End Of The Day... Channel your energy to create your future

Things are constantly vying for your attention. These distractions may pull you in different directions. The ideas that float through your mind are possibilities. Latch onto one that could change your world.

At The End Of The Day...

Are you listening to you?

_____

_____

_____

Where do you spend your energy?

_____

_____

_____

*At The End Of The Day...*If you see something wrong, do something

We are reminded to report a crime but what if it is not a crime but a hurt or sadness? Help someone if you can. Kindness matters! We need each other. Change is at the door. Open it.

At The End Of The Day...

Have you seen someone or something in need and helped?

_____
_____
_____

Change starts with us.

_____
_____
_____

At The End Of The Day... Each action has a consequence

There are so many ways to describe actions and consequences. It is important to understand how actions and consequences affect our lives. Bump your toe (action) and you may feel pain (consequence). Pay attention to the actions and consequences in your life. They matter.

At The End Of The Day...

What is the most recent action and consequence you experienced?

_____

_____

_____

How do you think actions and consequences matter?

_____

_____

_____

*At The End Of The Day...*A good cry can be good

There are times when a cry can be soul-cleansing. Whether you are crying because you are sad or crying because you are glad, let the tears fall. They can be good tears. When your cry is over, dry your eyes and leave the tears behind.

At The End Of The Day...

Do you cry often?

_____
_____
_____

Do you feel better after a cry?

_____
_____
_____

At The End Of The Day... A clean plate is not always a good thing

In years past, parents encouraged their children to clean their plates. With obesity ramped, we should eat carefully to ensure good health. Eat until you are full and then push the plate away. Check with your healthcare provider but eat around the aisle and eat healthy.

At The End Of The Day...

As a child, did you clean your plate?

_____

_____

_____

Do you purchase food from the outside the aisle?

_____

_____

_____

At The End Of The Day... No one knows your journey

Sometimes, we look at others and we wish we had their lives. As the saying goes, the grass is greener on the other side, but that is not always the case. Walk your journey. Give yourself grace in all you do. Everything will be alright. Your life is yours. Make it beautiful!

At The End Of The Day...

Have you wished you had someone else's life?
_____
_____
_____

How can you make your life better?
_____
_____
_____

At The End Of The Day... It is okay to say no

Sometimes, it is hard to say no. When we find ourselves pulled in so many different directions, sometimes saying no is challenging. Saying no is necessary for our mental well-being. Say no when you need to.

At The End Of The Day...

Do you find it difficult to say no?
_____
_____
_____

Who do find it difficult to say no?
_____
_____
_____

At The End Of The Day... You belong

At the death of Mr. George Floyd, attention was drawn to racial differences in America. Diversity, equity, and inclusion were the buzzwords of the day. Yet, belonging is important. Considering people need to belong wherever they are. Belonging is necessary.

At The End Of The Day...

Do you feel you belong?

_____

_____

_____

Why is belonging important?

_____

_____

_____

At The End Of The Day... We all have secrets

Sometimes we share our deepest thoughts with those we believe we can trust. And we later find that trust was misplaced. In some instances, those secrets are shared with others or used against you. Use good judgment before you share what is near and dear to you.

At The End Of The Day...

Has someone shared your secret(s)?

_____

_____

_____

Do you keep secrets?

_____

_____

_____

At The End Of The Day... Make yourself happy

Do not count on anyone else to make you happy. You are responsible for your happiness. Do whatever you can to make sure you are happy as much as you can. Others can contribute to your happiness, but you are the captain of your ship. Be happy!

At The End Of The Day...

Are you happy?

_____

_____

_____

Work on your happiness every day.

_____

_____

_____

At The End Of The Day... Give thanks for all things

We often take for granted all the blessings in our lives. Someone has it worse than you. Look around you, you are blessed. Throughout our lives, we have blessings and lessons. Appreciate and give thanks for both.

At The End Of The Day...

Do you see your blessings throughout the day?

_____

_____

_____

Do you learn from your lessons?

_____

_____

_____

*At The End Of The Day...*Move on from your mistakes

Acknowledge the mistakes and leave them behind. The more you wallow in them, the more power you give them. As I have said previously, we are not perfect. Everyone makes mistakes. Mistakes are necessary. The key is to move on.

At The End Of The Day...

How do you handle your mistakes?

_____

_____

_____

Forgive yourself when you make a mistake.

_____

_____

_____

At The End Of The Day... Plan to retire

We think of retirement as a joyous event. What will you do? Rest. Do nothing. Watch TV. Piddle. Read. Travel. After the euphoria of nothingness wears off, plan for what's next. It may be a year before you retire, come up with your next steps but have a plan.

At The End Of The Day...

Do you have a retirement plan?

_____

_____

_____

When will you retire?

_____

_____

_____

At The End Of The Day... Call your mother

If she is alive, she wants to hear your voice even if you call every day. If she is not alive, talk to her as if she were right beside you. The greatest gift a parent has is her child/children. Everyone is busy but there is always time for a call to or from your parents.

At The End Of The Day...

How often do you call your parents?

_____

_____

_____

Do you enjoy talking with your parents?

_____

_____

_____

At The End Of The Day... Pay your bills

If you do not have the money to pay your bills, call, or text your creditors. Putting your head in the sand does more to hurt than help you. Creditors believe people who do not pay their cost-to-live bills are not good credit risks. Call when you cannot pay.

At The End Of The Day...

What do you do when you do not have enough money to pay your bills?

_____

_____

_____

Call your creditors.

_____

_____

_____

At The End Of The Day... Animals love unconditionally

Animals come into our lives and ask only for food, water, and love. The love they give is beautiful. They come to us when we are sad, sick, or happy. They love to cuddle. They are our constant companion. You will never be lonely!

At The End Of The Day...

Do you have a pet?

_____

_____

_____

Do you know how your pet cares for you?

_____

_____

_____

*At The End Of The Day...*Loss is hard

Loss is difficult regardless of what, when, or how. Give yourself time to grieve. You may think you are over the loss and later the grief returns. This is normal. Be gentle with yourself. Allow yourself all the time you need to grieve.

At The End Of Day...

How do you express loss?

_____

_____

_____

Describe a loss you have experienced.

_____

_____

_____

At The End Of The Day... Do the work that brings you joy

Many of us work in a job or career that pays the bills, but we hate the work. When we work in a job we hate, it can be stressful and can lead to health issues. Find work that pays the bills and brings you joy.

At The End Of The Day...

Do you like the work you do?

_____

_____

_____

If money was no object, what would you do?

_____

_____

_____

*At The End Of Day...*Laugh often

Television is replete with commercials to rid our faces of wrinkles. There is a cheaper method... laughing. The more you laugh, the more you reduce lines in your face. Laughing will reduce stress and people around you will laugh too. Keep laughing.

At The End Of The Day...

How often do you laugh?

_____

_____

_____

When you laugh do you feel better?

_____

_____

_____

*At The End Of The Day...*Forgive yourself

Forgive others. Forgiveness helps you much more than it helps the person who caused the harm. Holding anger inside causes more harm to you than it does to the person who caused the harm. Forgive now and often. It is soul-soothing. Forgiving heals you.

At The End Of The Day...

Do you forgive?

_____

_____

_____

Forgive yourself and others often.

_____

_____

_____

*At The End Of The Day...*You get to choose who, what, when, and how

You do not have to answer the call, go to the event, hang out, eat the food, or do whatever. You get to choose. Do, go, or say what you want, respectfully. You have all the rights to your life.

At The End of The Day...

Do you feel you have to go out with friends?

_____

_____

_____

Do you block time just for you?

_____

_____

_____

At The End Of The Day... Anger is a demon

Short fuses do not serve us. Manage your temper. When you feel the urge to fly off the handle take a deep breath and count to ten. Reconsider the situation. Often anger takes us down a road that is difficult to manage. Breathe through your anger. Close your eyes and relax.

At The End Of The Day...

Are you easily angered?

_____

_____
_____

How do you manage anger?

_____

_____

_____

At The End Of The Day... Hold your head up high

You are a gift to the world. There is a place for you on this planet. As often as we are told we do not belong, we are different, bad, wrong, negative or whatever. Ignore the noise. It serves the person making the noise. Believe in you and carry on.

At The End Of The Day...

You belong.

_____

_____

_____

Stand up, head high.

_____

_____

_____

At The End Of The Day... Women matter

Women are the soul of the earth. Yet, our bodies fall prey to evil, those who wish to control it, force their will upon it, or abuse it. I ask that we acknowledge and recognize the importance of women and celebrate the beauty of women. If there is a woman in your life, celebrate her.

At The End Of The Day...

When you see other women, do you tell them how beautiful they are?

_____

_____

_____

Do you know how much women matter?

_____

_____

_____

At The End Of The Day... Make a plan and stick to it

It is often said, "Failing to plan is planning to fail." Start your plan by identifying the goal(s) of the plan and build from there. Stick to your plan. Allow for diversions but stay on course. Ask for help when needed. Return to the goal of your plan often.

At The End Of The Day...

Are you a planner?

_____

_____

_____

What do you do when your plan goes left?

_____

_____

_____

At The End Of The Day… Do not nag

However, be succinct in your point and leave it alone. Pushing the issue often turns the listener off. Let the listener know the issue is important to you and you wish to discuss it further when convenient.

At The End Of The Day...

Do you know how to get your issue addressed?

_____

_____

_____

Are you a nagger?

_____

_____

_____

At The End Of The Day... Be present

In today's multitasking life, being present is hard. Emails, phone calls, texts, work, family, social media, and everything else is vying for our attention. When we are with our family and friends, we need to focus on them. Tomorrow is not promised. Pay attention to your people.

At The End Of The Day...

Are you present with your family and friends?

_____

_____

_____

Do you find it difficult to be present?

_____

_____

_____

At The End Of The Day... There is room on the planet for us all

It is our responsibility to pave the way for young people, but we must remember our elders. The world is big enough for us all. Technology is moving so fast that older adults may find themselves on the outside looking in. Take care of everyone.

At The End Of The Day... Make the world you want

Others are happy to tell you what to think, how to think, and everything else. You were born with the mind as they were. Think for yourself. This world is made for everyone. Each of us can craft the world we want. Do not let others make it for you.

At The End Of The Day...

What would the world of your dream be?

_____

_____

_____

Go live the world of your dreams.

_____

_____

_____

At The End Of The Day... Be honest with your kids

They know way more than you think. Honest conversations go a long way. Once they leave the confines of our homes, they are no longer who we think they are. They know things we did not teach them. Trust them and they will trust us.

At The End Of The Day...

Do you have plain talks with your children?

_____

_____

_____

Share something real with your children.

_____

_____

_____

At The End Of The Day... Read a book

Reading a book has almost become obsolete. Many young people *read* social media. Digital print has become the go to source for reading. A book in your hand is a different experience. A book can take you to wonderful places. Read a book and enjoy the journey!

At The End Of The Day...

How often do you read a book?

_____

_____

_____

What do you like about reading a book?

_____

_____

_____

At The End Of The Day... There is nothing like a sharp-dressed person

There is nothing more stylish than a person dressed from head to toe. Dark suit, collared shirt, nice shoes, and just an air of sophistication. Casually dressed people are good too, it is just a suited people is sweet! Shout out to ZZ Top.

At The End Of The Day…

Do you like people dressed up or casually dressed?

_____

_____

_____

Do clothes make the person?

_____

_____

_____

At The End Of The Day... There is no sorry

No one should hit you period! Emotional, verbal, and physical abuses in relationships are unacceptable! Find a way out! When the abuser says they are sorry, do not believe it! Get out! It will happen again. Often after an abuse, the abuser says they are sorry, but the abuse continues. Please get out. Tell a friend. Tell someone! GET OUT!

At The End Of The Day...

Have you ever experienced relationship violence?

_____

_____

Do you know what to do when someone hurts you?

_____

_____

_____

At The End Of The Day... Be on time

When you are late, you delay the plans and schedules of those who depend on you. You Disrespect the time of the person who is waiting on you. You disrupt the day of the workflow. There are things you can do if you are going to be late, call, email, or text. Do not make being late a habit.

At The End Of The Day...

Are you late often?

_____

_____

_____

Do you understand the impact of being late?

_____

_____

_____

At The End Of The Day... It is never too late to start over

You can start over. Let the naysayers say what they may but push forward. You determine your what's next. If your body and mind are in good order, go for it! Try, try, and try again. Failure is great motivator.

At The End Of The Day...

Do you feel like you can do anything?

_____

_____

_____

Would you start over if you knew the outcome?

_____

_____

_____

At The End Of The Day... Hug a tree

It will hug you back for years to come. Trees save your life every day. They clean the air around us. Each fall, they give you a beautiful array of browns, yellows, and reds. Trees are simply amazing. If you must cut down a tree, plant a new one. Hug a tree.

At The End Of The Day...

Are you a tree person?

_____

_____

_____

What are your favorite things about trees?

_____

_____

_____

At The End Of The Day... A person of color is any person

We are all people of color. Labeling people disables people. As a society, we tend to categorize things...dogs, trees, cars, and people. This makes some sense but when it is done to minimize people, it hurts us all. How about we just call people humans?

At The End Of Day...

How do you see yourself?

_____

_____

_____

Do you believe labels are good?

_____

_____

_____

*At The End Of The Day...*If no one else will hug you, hug yourself

Self-love is a deep and complete love. It does not have conditions. Often, we struggle to find love. Love has ups and downs. Self-esteem takes hits, and it causes us to doubt ourselves. When we are down and unsure, take a moment to hug and love yourself.

At The End Of The Day...

Do you practice self-love?

_____

_____

_____

At the end of every day, hug yourself.

_____

_____

_____

At The End Of The Day... Children are the purest form of innocence

Sometimes, adults corrupt the purity of children with their bias. At our core, most humans are good people. If you can, allow children to develop their views of the world. Let our children see the good in humanity. We need each other. Let us get know each other beyond labels.

At The End Of The Day...

How do children learn about each other?

_____

_____

_____

How can we make the world a better place?

_____

_____

_____

At The End Of The Day... We have no idea of the power of our tongues and eyes

It is said, the tongue has the power of life and death. The eyes also have the power to do damage. The damage they do can often take years or in some instances cannot be undone. Be judicial in how you speak and treat others. Speak love!

At The End Of The Day...

Has someone said something to hurt you?

_____

_____

_____

Do you know the power of the tongue?

_____

_____

_____

At The End Of The Day... Have multiple streams of income

Having a job is a good thing but you are at the mercy of your employer. Have more than one source of income. Young people call that a side hustle. Have a few side hustles (all legal). Many athletes have multiple side hustles. Let them be your example. Hustle on.

At The End Of The Day...

Do you have a second income?

_____

_____

_____

Are thinking of retiring?

_____

_____

_____

At The End Of The Day... Take your time with you

We are always in a hurry. We rarely take time to appreciate ourselves. We rush through our baths. We eat in a hurry. We have so much to do. Slow down with you. Enjoy your bath and food. Take time each day to see and appreciate you.

At The End Of Day...

When was the last time you noticed you?

_____

_____

_____

Slow down, you may find things about yourself you did not know.

_____

_____

_____

At The End Of The Day... Plastic Smiles

Often people smile at you with these concocted smiles that make you think the person who is smiling at you is genuine. Be wary of these people. You may not be safe. The smile may be hiding another intent. The voice often conveys the intent. Be careful.

At The End Of The Day...

Can you sense plastic people?

_____

_____

_____

Are you a good judge of people?

_____

_____

_____

At The End Of The Day...
Being wealthy will not make you happy

You can buy a lot of material things. However, happiness is an emotion. It does not fit in a shoe, a car, or a house. We make our happiness. It can be found within you and the work you do with you. Start small. Simple things generally make us happy.

At The End Of The Day...

Do you know what makes you happy?

_____

_____

_____

Where is your happy place?

_____

_____

_____

At The End Of The Day...
Public education deserve better than a lottery ticket

Public education budgets have been slashed and slashed. Yet, public education is our best hope for an equitable society. Society needs public education for people to see each other as humans.

At The End Of The Day...

Do you believe in public education?

_____

_____

_____

Did you receive a public education?

_____

_____

_____

At The End Of The Day... Be kind to others

Kindness is the golden ticket. Hold the door open for the person in front or behind you. A kind gesture may help someone have a good day. When we show kindness, it makes us feel better. A little kindness goes a long way. We all win when kindness is our intention.

At The End Of The Day....

Have you been kind today?

_____

_____

_____

Has someone shown you kindness?

_____

_____

_____

At The End Of The Day... Read the fine print

Ads offer great deals. They have celebrities marketing the product, or a slick campaign. Be wary. If it looks or sounds too good to be true, it probably is. Read before you agree, buy, or sign up. Half off of what? The devil is in the details.

At The End Of The Day....

Have fell for a gotcha?

_____

_____

_____

Do you trust commercials?

_____

_____

_____

At The End Of The Day... A good father is a gift

Many women lack the benefit of a father. Thank you to all the fathers who step up every day. To the girls without fathers, you have and can managed without one thus far. Good job! Do not look for a father in the men you date. You have taken care of you this far. Trust and love you first and most.

At The End Of The Day...

How do fathers impact their daughters' life?

_____

_____

_____

Do you think fathers matters in a girl's life?

_____

_____

_____

At The End Of The Day... Anything you chase will run

It has been said, if you chase a dog, it will run. This phrase can be applied to love. If you want romance, do not chase it. The better hack is to ignore it. Let the romance simmer. There is a person for you. Have patience grasshopper.

At The End Of The Day...

Have you ever chased a love interest?

_____

_____

_____

Do you have the patience to wait for love?

_____

_____

_____

At The End Of The Day... Time heals

Time is not measured by our senses. Time comes at its appropriate time. Waiting is not fun, but it has a purpose. Waiting teaches us patience. As we wait, the healing process begins, and we find new interests. Allow time its purpose.

At The End Of The Day...

Do you want everything right now?

_____

_____

_____

Do you appreciate the benefit of waiting?

_____

_____

_____

At The End Of The Day... Save the planet

Many argue the planet temperature is not rising. This is our planet. It will only survive if you care for it. Do your part. Recycle. Do not litter. Use less water. Drive clean. Caring for the planet is not easy but we can do it. Some things are simple and others not so much. But do your part. Leave a better planet for our children.

At The End Of Day...

How can you save the planet?

_____

_____

_____

Do you believe the planet is in peril?

_____

_____

_____

At The End Of The Day... Reach across the aisle

Most times, we only work with the people on our team. Yet, there are people just on the other side of the aisle who may be valuable. It may be helpful to include those beyond your team. Build a community of diverse team members across the aisle and you may find just what you need.

At The End Of The Day...

Have you ever included others beyond your team?

_____

_____

_____

Do you work collaboratively?

_____

_____

_____

At The End Of The Day...

This journal is a collection of my blessings, experiences, and lessons. I hope these idioms assist in your journey. In all things, take good care of yourself. Offer forgiveness and grace to yourself and others in all that you do. TAKE GOOD CARE.

...It Is The End Of The Day!

Made in the USA
Columbia, SC
07 October 2023

33a811f3-0324-45ef-9bb8-b03a5592baceR01